D0339914

the peril of magnificent love

the peril of magnificent love

emma magenta

**Andrews McMeel
Publishing**

Kansas City

07 08 LEO 10 9 8 7 6 5 4 3

ISBN-13:978-0-7407-4804-2

ISBN-10:0-7407-4804-1

Library of Congress Control Number: 2004103262

Book design by Timothy Clift

ATTENTION: SCHOOLS AND BUSINESSES

Andrews McMeel books are available at quantity discounts with bulk purchase for educational, business, or sales promotional use. For information, please write to: Special Sales Department, Andrews McMeel Publishing, LLC, an Andrews McMeel Universal company, 4520 Main Street, Kansas City, Missouri 64111.

to my sister anne,
who just seems to understand.

acknowledgments

to bradley trevor greive and deborah bibby for their enormous faith in me, and their support. thank you so much. i feel really honored to be working with two people who possess such vision and integrity.

also to tim clift for his incredible dedication, patience, and exquisite crafting of my little book.

now a big gorgeous tick and thank you goes to liza eisserman, david lennon, and sascha horler. each of these little darlings provided enormous encouragement and tangible support to me with my work from day one.

to the berkelouw family, in particular paul for putting up with my constant decoration of his shop in paddington. also to the gorgeous staff at berkelouw books, who tolerate my need to draw on everything (even them).

to my darling mum, dad, anne, and dan for being the impetus for my exploration of the inane.

to my brilliant friends who have answered all my "cooeee" moments with love and encouragement: louwe, roxana, sonia, maggie, raquel, tony, simon, budda, falador (especially for your advice), and pamela.

contra-mestre peixe of group capoeira brasil for the gift of capoeira and the encouragement of everyone in the group.

the pursuit of divine union
can be a tricky quest.

magenta had as her fortune the
company of exquisite companions,

a favorite tree,

and a passion for break dancing.

so one can forgive her naive assumption that
despite his penchant for wearing bad shoes,
his arrival in her life was a promise of further joy.

in his warm hands she found the key to
infinite bliss while the beauty of his countenance
promised a life of eternal rapture.

overcome by these new delights, she made an
invocation of gratitude to the supreme deity for
creating a situation where her biggest love,

deepest secrets,

and superb eccentricities

were soon to be understood
by a perfect other.

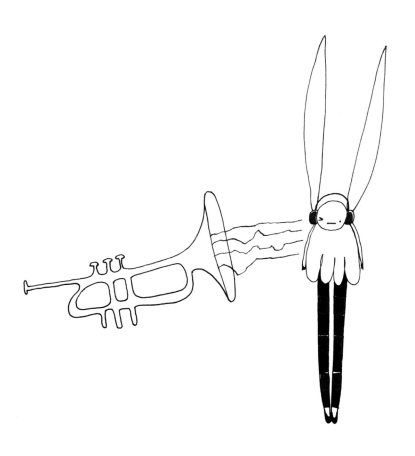

in response to her praise, a victorious
big-band trumpet mysteriously sounded,

as she saw in his eyes a brilliant signal for a
completely new world to which she happily absconded.

for such an adventure, she felt it only appropriate to
pack her largest suitcase with sustaining provisions,

and at the very least adorn a pair of fresh socks.

there was no room for her tree, but she lifted its spirits with the promise of continuous kisses on their next meeting.

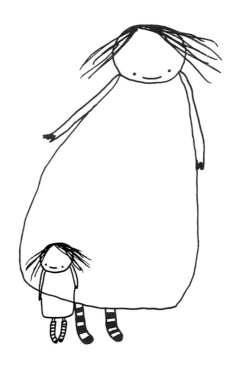

after a while her big feelings for him
made her grow to such enormous proportions
that she soon left herself behind.

her friends too became obsolete as companions
and served only as ears to hear about this love.

this magnificent love!

the love that forced her to buy new undies,

swing naked from chandeliers,

and shake in public places from too much feeling.

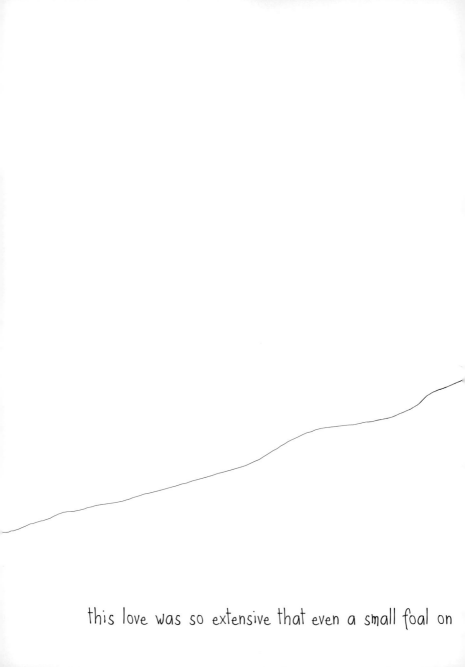

this love was so extensive that even a small foal on

vacation at the north pole knew about it and felt overwhelmed.

all things were suspended in its glittering splendor.

she longed to tell him of these exploding emotions,
but suddenly she felt afraid,

and to say the least, trés vulnerable.

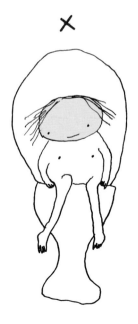

it occurred to her that maybe dancing would help.

it's true

as if by sheer serendipity a passing stranger
suggested the canadian three-step was a particularly
effective method of healing one's inner fool.

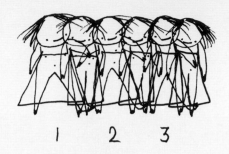

1   2   3

Spin

Kick

feeling more secure in herself, she decided to wear a brave dress to see if he would notice the size of her heart.

he didn't.

finding herself alone in the dark,
she searched blindly for solace and inspiration.

after some time,
she stumbled upon the thrill of wearing gorgeous boots,

and not long after,
the gentle fulfillment that comes from patting a quail.

feeling a little more hopeful again, she decided
that new hair might effectively showcase her
true feelings and inner desires.

then again, perhaps it wouldn't.

= stress

in the end, she nestled into a red hunting hat
and hibernated through a self-imposed winter.

awakening refreshed but still a little shaken, she knew
that to be victorious her next move had to be flawless.

so to avoid any possible faux pas,
she presented him with a box of generous proportions
containing her many different selves.

he had only to make his selection.

trés belle.

spontaneous.

übersmart.

philosophical.

good at dinner parties.

deep.

unfortunately, she failed to establish that
only one selection was possible at a time,

goody

and yet she was still victorious.

for a while at least.

until it started.

first, the inertia,

then the video nights,

the waiting for real moments together,

interspersed with betrayal,

deception,

and mind games.

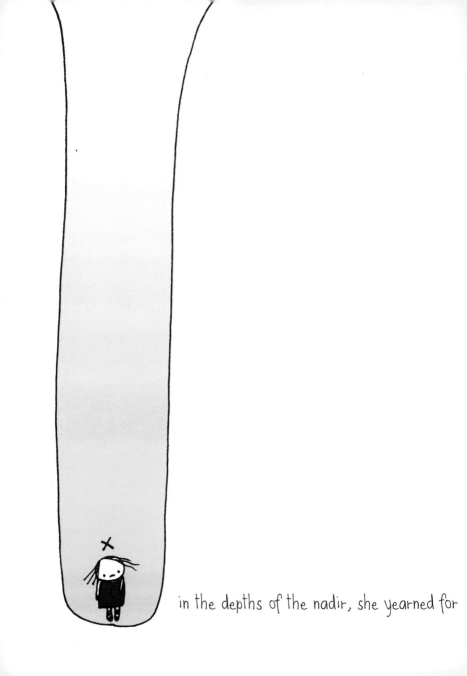

in the depths of the nadir, she yearned for

an existence unencumbered by this smorgasbord of lo-fi moments.

so she ruminated through her options

and imagined her life if she were to
continue on in the same manner,

if she tried to analyze the problem
in the advent of a solution,

or perhaps if she left altogether.

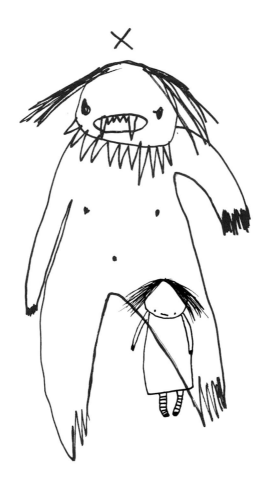

before her shadow self could take over entirely,

she took herself to a cliff top where she sang
a little song to a norse god for guidance.

within the hour she was blessed
with a moment of unprecedented clarity.

and with epic silence,
she concluded that perhaps she had idealized him.

a group of familiar onlookers gathered in
humble appreciation to witness her
first sane thought in years.

suddenly the life she had known prior to this romantic
misadventure was imbued with the scent of possibility.

her friends seemed funnier than she remembered,

her tree was more charming than ever,

and everything seemed to move to the pulse of an
invisible samba beat, making her swell with joy.

and with a strange sense of liberty,

she became the person she was looking for.